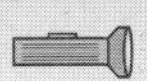

MyReportLinks.com Books

Tools Search Notes Discuss Go!

OREGON

A MyReportLinks.com Book

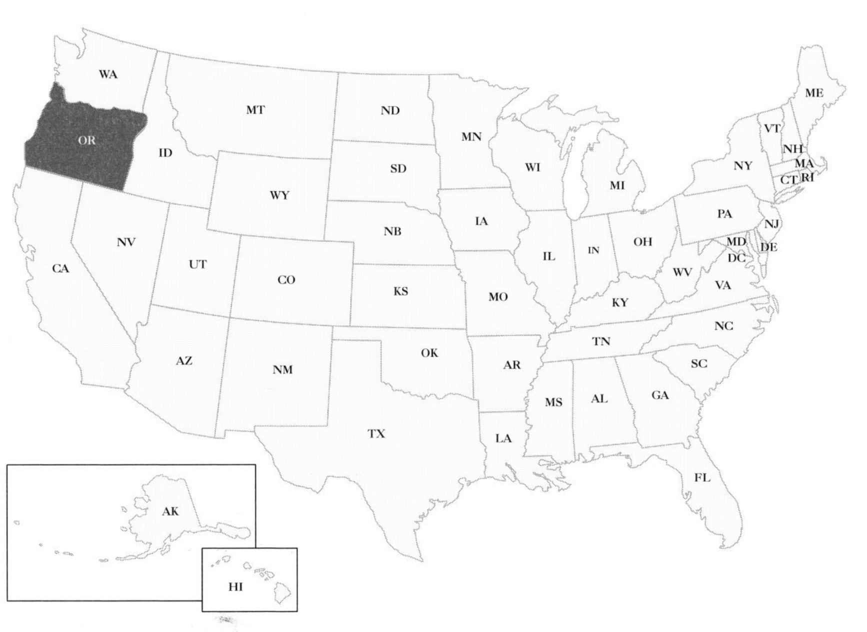

Ron Knapp

MyReportLinks.com Books

an imprint of

Enslow Publishers, Inc.

Box 398, 40 Industrial Road
Berkeley Heights, NJ 07922
USA

For Cory Cohoon, who made it all the way to Oregon

MyReportLinks.com Books, an imprint of Enslow Publishers, Inc. MyReportLinks is a trademark of Enslow Publishers, Inc.

Library of Congress Cataloging-in-Publication Data

Knapp, Ron.
Oregon / Ron Knapp.
p. cm. — (States)
Contents: The state of Oregon — Land and climate — Interesting Oregonians — Government and economy — History.
Includes bibliographical references and index.
ISBN 0-7660-5021-1
1. Oregon—Juvenile literature. [1. Oregon.] I. Title. II. States (Series : Berkeley Heights, N.J.)
F876.3 .K58 2002
979.5—dc21
2002007479

Printed in the United States of America

10 9 8 7 6 5 4 3 2 1

To Our Readers:
Through the purchase of this book, you and your library gain access to the Report Links that specifically back up this book.
The Publisher will provide access to the Report Links that back up this book and will keep these Report Links up to date on **www.myreportlinks.com** for three years from the book's first publication date.
We have done our best to make sure all Internet addresses in this book were active and appropriate when we went to press. However, the author and the Publisher have no control over, and assume no liability for, the material available on those Internet sites or on other Web sites they may link to.
The usage of the MyReportLinks.com Books Web site is subject to the terms and conditions stated on the Usage Policy Statement on **www.myreportlinks.com**.
In the future, a password may be required to access the Report Links that back up this book. The password is found on the bottom of page 4 of this book.
Any comments or suggestions can be sent by e-mail to comments@myreportlinks.com or to the address on the back cover.

Photo Credits: © Copyright 1995 PhotoDisc, Inc., pp. 17, 18, 21; © Corel Corporation, pp. 3, 10; America's Story from America's Library/Library of Congress, p. 13; Enslow Publishers, Inc., pp. 1, 15; Feminist Voices & Visions from the Pacific, p. 28; MyReportLinks.com Books, p. 4; New Perspectives on the West/PBS, p. 27; NewOregonTrail.com, p. 22; Notable American Unitarians/Harvard Square Library, p. 30; Oregon Blue Book, pp. 32, 34, 35; Oregon State Archives, pp. 12, 24, 43; The Corps/PBS, pp. 39, 40; The Oregon Trail/PBS, p. 25.

Cover Photo: © Copyright 1999 PhotoDisc, Inc.

Cover Description: Crater Lake

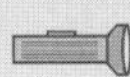

Contents

MyReportLinks.com Books

Great Books, Great Links, Great for Research!

MyReportLinks.com Books present the information you need to learn about your report subject. In addition, they show you where to go on the Internet for more information. The pre-evaluated Report Links that back up this book are kept up to date on **www.myreportlinks.com**. With the purchase of a MyReportLinks.com Books title, you and your library gain access to the Report Links that specifically back up that book. The Report Links save hours of research time and link to dozens—even hundreds—of Web sites, source documents, and photos related to your report topic.

Please see "To Our Readers" on the Copyright page for important information about this book, the MyReportLinks.com Books Web site, and the Report Links that back up this book.

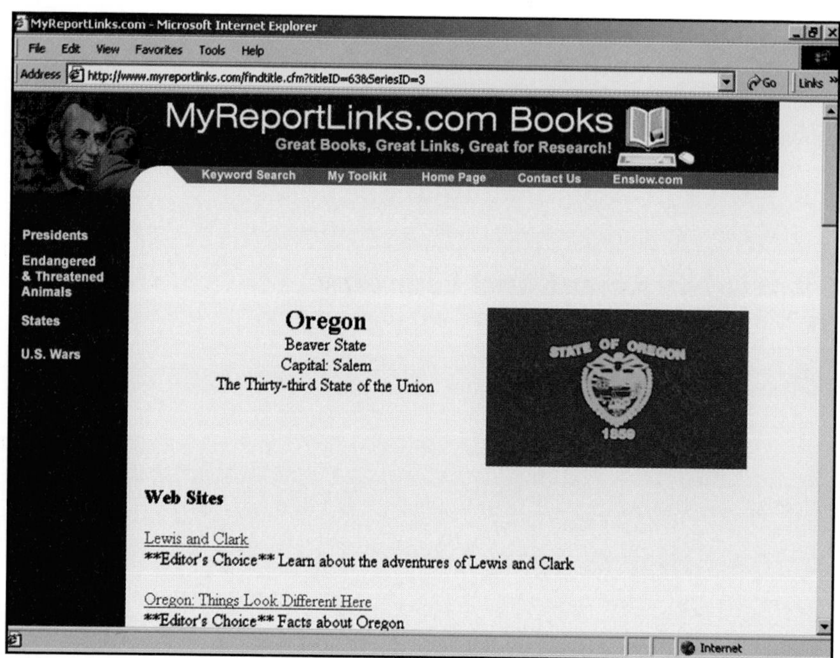

Access:

The Publisher will provide access to the Report Links that back up this book and will try to keep these Report Links up to date on our Web site for three years from the book's first publication date. Please enter **SOR1149** if asked for a password.

Report Links

The Internet sites described below can be accessed at http://www.myreportlinks.com

*Editor's choice

▶ Lewis and Clark

This comprehensive site about Lewis and Clark offers information about their travels, the members of their corps, their legacy, and much more.

Link to this Internet site from http://www.myreportlinks.com

*Editor's choice

▶ Oregon: Things Look Different Here

At this Web site you will find information about Oregon's geography, government, people, history, maps, statistics, tourist information, and more.

Link to this Internet site from http://www.myreportlinks.com

*Editor's choice

▶ 50th Anniversary Exhibit Home Page

This Web site from the Oregon State Archives offers online illustrated exhibits relating to the history of Oregon, including Oregon Environment, Oregon Constitution, and Graphic Arts Drawings.

Link to this Internet site from http://www.myreportlinks.com

*Editor's choice

▶ In Search of the Oregon Trail

At this site you will find Oregon Trail myths, trivia, maps, a time line, and more.

Link to this Internet site from http://www.myreportlinks.com

*Editor's choice

▶ Oregon.gov

This comprehensive site, brought to you by the state of Oregon, offers information about the state's history, geography, economy, and much more.

Link to this Internet site from http://www.myreportlinks.com

*Editor's choice

▶ Congress Created the Oregon Territory

America's Story from America's Library, a Library of Congress Web site, provides a brief history of when Congress declared Oregon a territory.

Link to this Internet site from http://www.myreportlinks.com

Report Links

The Internet sites described below can be accessed at
http://www.myreportlinks.com

▶Applegate Trail: Southern Route of the Oregon Trail
This Web site offers the history of Applegate Trail, maps, biographies of those who took the trail, as well as links to other resources about Oregon.

Link to this Internet site from http://www.myreportlinks.com

▶Chief Joseph
At this PBS Web site you will find the biography of Chief Joseph, who was born in Wallowa Valley, Oregon.

Link to this Internet site from http://www.myreportlinks.com

▶Chief Joseph Surrenders
This page contains Nez Percé Chief Joseph's speech surrendering to the United States Army in 1877. Information on the conflict with the Nez Percé is also provided.

Link to this Internet site from http://www.myreportlinks.com

▶Discover Cathlapotle!
This site offers articles about people, places, culture, and events of the Chinook Indians.

Link to this Internet site from http://www.myreportlinks.com

▶Explore the States: Oregon
America's Story from America's Library, a Library of Congress Web site, provides an overview of interesting facts and historical information about the state of Oregon. You will also find links to other stories about Oregon.

Link to this Internet site from http://www.myreportlinks.com

▶Feminist Voices & Visions: Abigail Scott Duniway
This comprehensive site offers biographical information, photographs, and other resources related to Abigail Scott Duniway, the woman who played a major role in the suffrage movement of the Pacific Northwest.

Link to this Internet site from http://www.myreportlinks.com

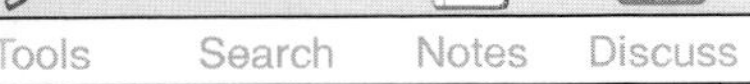

Report Links

The Internet sites described below can be accessed at
http://www.myreportlinks.com

▶ History & Culture of the Cayuse, Umatilla and Walla Walla Indians

At this Web site you can explore the history, culture, and traditions of Umatilla, Cayuse, and Walla Walla Indians.

Link to this Internet site from http://www.myreportlinks.com

▶ Historical Gazette

This site offers historic newspaper articles about subjects such as gold seekers, the Oregon Trail, Chief Joseph, and women's suffrage.

Link to this Internet site from http://www.myreportlinks.com

▶ Maurine Neuberger: United States Senator

This obituary offers a comprehensive biography of Maurine Neuberger that includes her political career, personal life, education, and more.

Link to this Internet site from http://www.myreportlinks.com

▶ The McLoughlin House

At this Web site you will learn about Dr. John McLoughlin and his contributions to Oregon's early history.

Link to this Internet site from http://www.myreportlinks.com

▶ New Perspectives on The West

This PBS Web site offers maps of Oregon, information about Chief Joseph and the Nez Percé Indians, maps of Wallowa Valley, maps of trails and territories, and information about historic people, places, and events of the West.

Link to this Internet site from http://www.myreportlinks.com

▶ On This Day in Oregon

At this Web site you can explore Oregon's history by reading what happened on each day of the year.

Link to this Internet site from http://www.myreportlinks.com

The Internet sites described below can be accessed at **http://www.myreportlinks.com**

▶Oregon

This site contains a comprehensive history of Oregon that dates from 10,000 B.C. to the present. You will also learn about Oregon lighthouses, wilderness, rivers, and more.

Link to this Internet site from http://www.myreportlinks.com

▶Oregon Blue Book: Notables–Charles McNary

This page offers a short biography of Charles McNary, the Oregon senator who was minority leader for over a decade and ran for vice president in 1940 on the Wendell Wilkie ticket.

Link to this Internet site from http://www.myreportlinks.com

▶Oregon Coast Aquarium

At this Web site you learn all about marine life at the Oregon Coast Aquarium, including birds, fish, invertebrates, and marine mammals.

Link to this Internet site from http://www.myreportlinks.com

▶Oregon Pioneers

This comprehensive site offers profiles of early explorers, American Indians, prominent fur traders, and missionaries. Journals, diaries, photos, and emigrant lists are also available.

Link to this Internet site from http://www.myreportlinks.com

▶Oregon State Parks and Recreation: Visiting State Parks

This site offers information about Oregon State parks, historic sites, visitor information, and more.

Link to this Internet site from http://www.myreportlinks.com

▶The Oregon Trail

This site offers history, sites, facts, memoirs, maps, and other resources of the Oregon Trail.

Link to this Internet site from http://www.myreportlinks.com

Report Links

The Internet sites described below can be accessed at **http://www.myreportlinks.com**

▶ Oregon Trail Time Frame

This comprehensive site offers a year-by-year description of travelers and events along the Oregon Trail between 1792 and 1843. A map of the trail can be downloaded.

Link to this Internet site from http://www.myreportlinks.com

▶ Phil Knight: The Force Behind Nike

This biographical feature article about Nike founder and CEO Phil Knight discusses his youth, company, and how he revolutionized the athletic shoe industry.

Link to this Internet site from http://www.myreportlinks.com

▶ Stately Knowledge: Oregon

At this Web site you will find facts and figures on the state of Oregon. There are also links to other articles with information about Oregon.

Link to this Internet site from http://www.myreportlinks.com

▶ Uncomfortable History: The Whitman Massacre

This article from the *Seattle Times* discusses the lives and accomplishments of Marcus and Narcissa Whitman, and the legacy of the Whitman massacre.

Link to this Internet site from http://www.myreportlinks.com

▶ Welcome to Oregon

This comprehensive site offers cultural, historical, and geographical facts, maps, and links related to the state of Oregon.

Link to this Internet site from http://www.myreportlinks.com

▶ Welcome to the End of the Oregon Trail

At the End of the Oregon Trail Web site you will find maps, emigrant biographies, pioneer diaries, time lines, articles, and information about touring the Oregon Trail.

Link to this Internet site from http://www.myreportlinks.com

Oregon Facts

Capital
Salem

Gained Statehood
February 14, 1859

Population
3,421,399*

Bird
Western meadowlark

Tree
Douglas fir

Flower
Oregon grape

Mammal
Beaver

Insect
Swallowtail butterfly

Fish
Chinook salmon

Rock
Thunderegg

Gemstone
Sunstone

Song
"Oregon, My Oregon" Words by J. A. Buchanan; music by Henry B. Murtagh.

Motto
Alis volat Propriis (Latin for "She flies with her own wings")

Nickname
The Beaver State

Flag
The Oregon flag is blue and gold, with images on both sides. An image of a beaver is on the back. On the front is a shield with an eagle on top, and the words "The Union." There are thirty-three stars because Oregon was the thirty-third state. Images of wheat, a pickax, and a plow represent Oregon's mining and farming industries. There are two ships, a British ship leaving the area, and an American ship that is arriving. It symbolizes the rise of the United States' power in the area.

**Population reflects the 2000 census.*

Chapter 1 ▶

The Beaver State

Oregon must be a very special place. Almost half a million people walked and drove covered wagons halfway across a continent to get there. You can see one of their covered wagons on the state flag. The travelers walked 2,000 miles across plains and mountains to get to their new home. In the 1800s, the Oregon Trail was a busy place.

The settlers found a land covered with forests. If they wanted to farm, they had to cut down acres of trees. Later, the lumber companies came in and did the same thing for profit. The rich soil has supported farms for generations.

The woods were home to deer, elk, and other game that supplied meat for the early Oregonians. Lakes, rivers, and the Pacific Ocean are filled with fish.

The state's name probably comes from the word *Ouragan*, which at one time was the name given to the Columbia River. In French, *Ouragan* means hurricane. The big river must have seemed rough and unpredictable to the earliest settlers. Today, the word comes to mind when tourists travel the wild white-water rapids of the Snake River through the steep walls of Hell's Canyon.

Oregon is better known for its quiet beauty. Its early white settlers could not help being awed by the mountains, streams, cliffs, and forests. After walking across miles and miles of the plains, snowcapped peaks such as Mount Hood were a gorgeous, welcome sight.

The lava beds in the southern part of the state are stark, but lovely. The craggy rocks along the Pacific coast offer the perfect spot for watching a quiet sunset. Of course, there are also the trees. Millions and millions of them. Half of Oregon is still covered by forests.

Better Nicknames

Over the years, Oregonians have tried to come up with more appropriate nicknames for their state other than hurricane. Because of the state's natural beauty, Pacific Wonderland seems to fit. Forest State is also a good title for a place half-covered by trees.

One of the most unusual names is The Beaver State. The first small groups of white settlers who came to the area were not looking for good farmlands or natural

Oregon is known for its natural beauty. Many Oregonians take pride in preserving their state's environment.

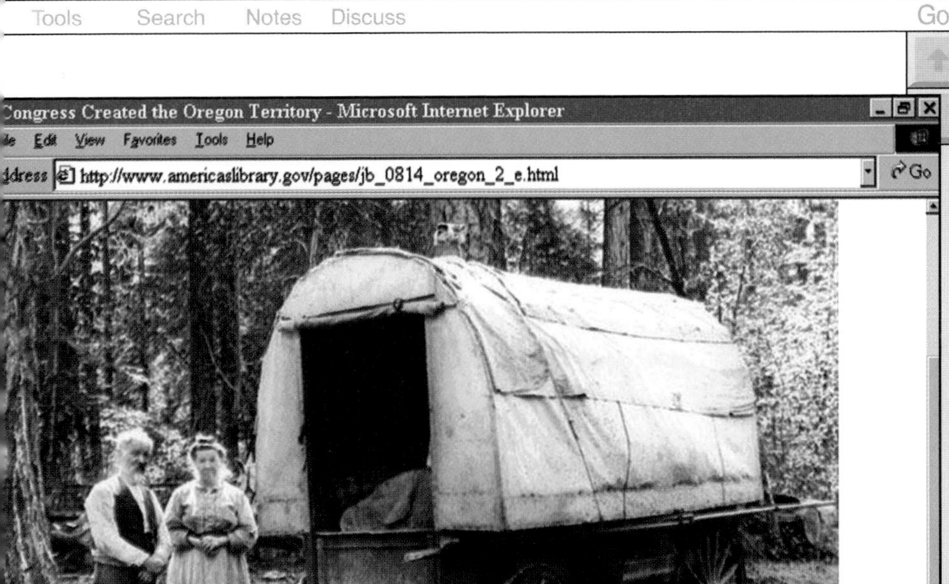

Most people who traveled from the Midwest to Oregon did so in a covered wagon.

beauty. They wanted beaver pelts. Fortunes were made by trapping the animal, trading the furs, and transporting them to the people in cities who wanted them.

The People

Almost all of the pioneers who traveled the Oregon Trail were white. The American Indians who had lived in Oregon for centuries were quickly displaced. Many of them were moved to less desirable land on reservations in Idaho or Oklahoma. Thousands died from diseases brought by the new settlers.

Since then, Oregon's population has remained predominately white. It is one of the least diverse states in the nation. According to the 2000 census, 86.6 percent of Oregon's population is white. The largest minority group is Asian Americans, who make up just 3 percent of the total. African Americans total 1.6 percent of the population, and American Indians make up 1.3 percent.

Most of Oregon's approximately 3.5 million people live in Portland and in medium-sized urban areas such as Salem, Corvallis, and Eugene that stretch down the Willamette Valley in the northwest corner of the state.

Chapter 2 ▶

Land and Climate

Oregon is divided unevenly by the Cascade Mountains. Tallest of these in Oregon is Mount Hood, which is 11,239 feet high. Other peaks almost that high are Mount Jefferson, the Three Sisters, and Mount McLoughlin.

Two-thirds of the state lies to the east of the mountains. It is a relatively flat area known as the Columbia Plateau. It was formed thousands of years ago when lava

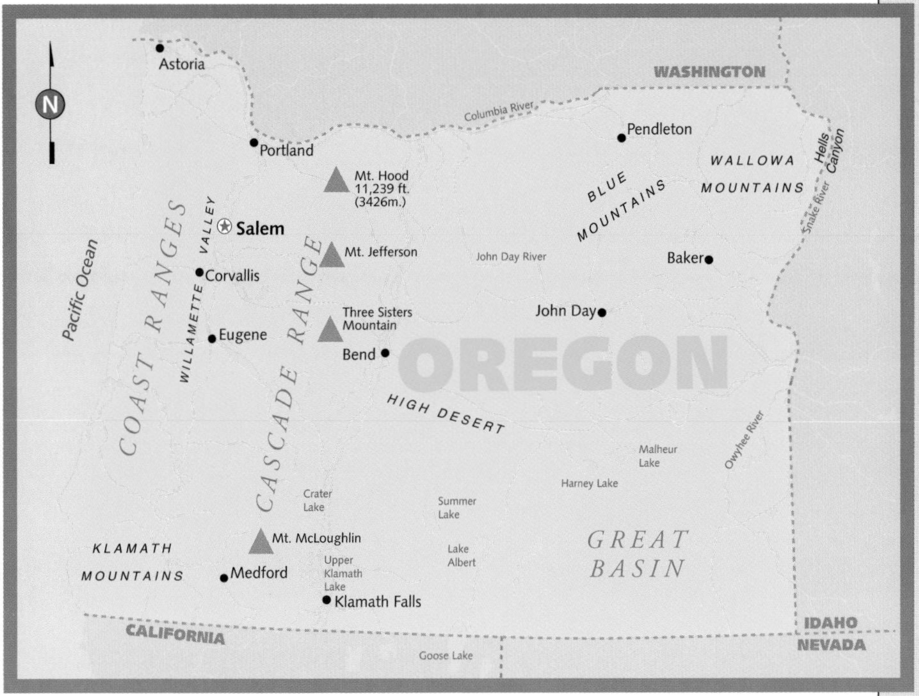

A map of Oregon.

poured out of cracks in the ground. The eruptions did not reach all the high spots. There are still some rugged mountains on the plateau.

On the western edge of the Cascades is the Willamette Valley, where most Oregonians live. This is a narrow strip of fertile land bordered on the west by the Coast Range, a series of small mountains on the edge of the Pacific Ocean.

The Basin and Range Region, south of the Columbia Plateau, is a dry, flat, mostly empty area. The Klamath Mountains, located in the southwest corner of the state, are covered by thick forests.

The Climate

It usually does not get very warm or very cold in Oregon. During July and August, the hottest summer months, average temperatures range between 58°F and 79°F. For a state as far north as Oregon, the winter weather is surprisingly mild. Warm Pacific winds help to keep it comfortable. Even in January, the coldest month, temperatures range from 35°F to 44°F at lower elevations.

The breezes from the ocean also have an effect on precipitation. When the moist winds first encounter land on the coast, they drop a great deal rain and snow. Some coastal areas receive as much as 130 inches of precipitation a year. As the winds move farther inland, they are drier, resulting in less rain and snow. The eastern Columbia Plateau is the driest part of the state.

Portland

The Chinook Indians liked to camp at a flat area near the point where the Columbia and Willamette rivers meet. Over the years, they cut down about an acre of the forest for firewood.

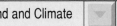

Although Portland is a bustling city, the people of Portland are careful to not overdevelop the area. Today, there are more than two hundred parks in the city.

When the white settlers arrived, the cleared area was a perfect spot for a settlement. Because of all the tree stumps left by the Chinook, Asa Lovejoy and Francis Pettygrove nicknamed their town Stumptown.

In 1845, they decided they wanted a new name. Each man wanted to name the settlement after his hometown. Pettygrove was from Portland, Maine; Lovejoy was from Boston, Massachusetts. They flipped a coin. Pettygrove won. Stumptown became Portland, Oregon.

As their city grew, the people of Portland wanted to ensure that they could continue to enjoy the area's natural beauty. Today, there are more than two hundred parks in the city. Forest Park covers 4,800 acres. South Park Blocks is a boulevard in the middle of the downtown area, filled

with trees, grass, and gardens. The newest green area is Gov. Tom McCall Waterfront Park. It was formed by digging up a highway on the banks of the Willamette River. Today joggers, rollerbladers, and picnickers have replaced traffic jams.

Not all the city's parks are large. The world's smallest park is in Portland. Mills End Park is just a tiny square traffic island that measures about two feet across. It was created as a joke on St. Patrick's Day in 1948 as a home for leprechauns.

Portland, with a population of 529,121, is by far the biggest city in Oregon. It has almost four times as many people as Eugene, the next largest city.

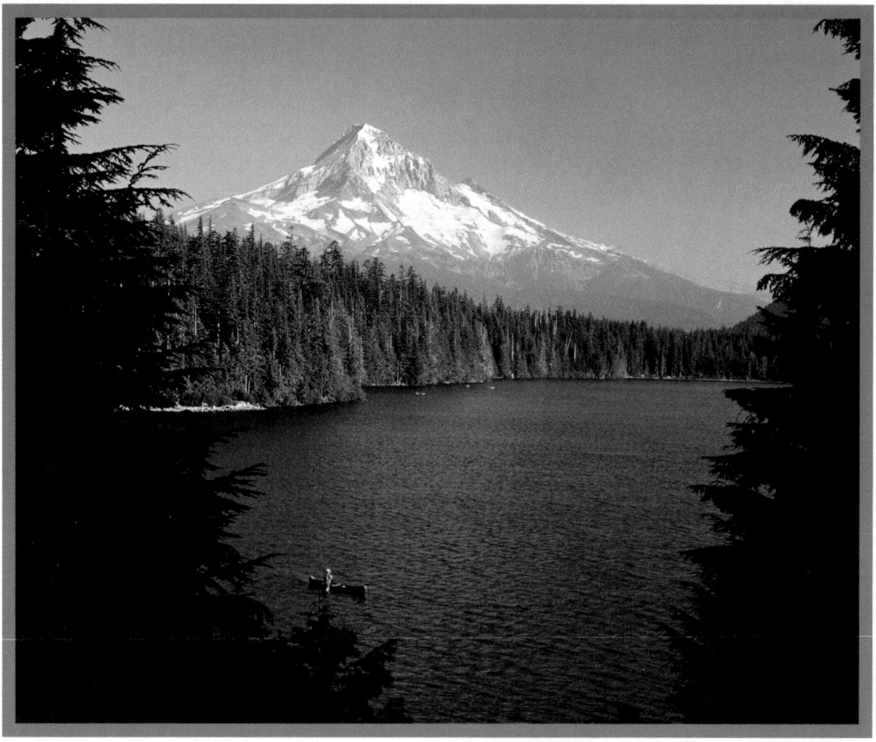

Mount Hood is the tallest mountain in Oregon, reaching over 11,000 feet. It can be seen from almost anywhere in Portland.

The people of Portland do not want to lose their view of the mountains. Therefore, no building over forty stories can be erected. That means that beautiful Mount Hood can be seen from almost every part of the city.

Places to Visit

At the National Historic Oregon Trail Interpretive Center, volunteers dressed as pioneers explain life on the Oregon Trail and in the new territory. They use exhibits and artifacts to demonstrate the struggles of the early white settlers. There are plays and a recreated pioneer camp.

The center is located near Baker City, one of the first spots on the Oregon Trail that is actually in Oregon. Covered wagons scratched out wheel ruts in the soft rock around Baker City. Fifteen miles of the ruts are still there today.

John McLoughlin, the father of Oregon, built his last home in 1845. Today the John McLoughlin House National Historical Site still contains most of the original furnishings. The house is in Oregon City, where the Oregon Trail ended at Willamette Falls.

Oregon has always been known for its wooden covered bridges. Its earliest white settlers put roofs on bridges to protect them from rain and keep the wood from rotting. The roofs also made the bridges convenient places for dances and meetings.

Many of the bridges have been replaced by modern steel and concrete models, but there are still about fifty covered wooden bridges in the state. Lost Creek Bridge, in Jackson County, is the shortest at just 39 feet long. Office Bridge, in Lane County, at 180 feet, is the longest.

Ashland is almost halfway around the world from London, England, where William Shakespeare produced his plays. That has not stopped this small city from becoming the home of the Oregon Shakespeare Festival. Tragedies, comedies, and histories are performed in a pair of indoor theaters, as well as on an outdoor stage modeled after Shakespeare's own Globe Theater.

Caves

Oregon Caves National Monument is deep within the Siskiyou Mountains. Because it is a cave, the temperature, no matter the season, is always close to 40°F. A walk through the caves is a strenuous journey. There are more than five hundred stairs along the way. You cannot go in without a guide.

Still, it is a wonderful walk. Over thousands of years, underground streams have carved out huge rooms in the limestone. Some are sixty feet high and almost as long as a football field. Stalactites hang from the ceiling. The rock formations bear such colorful names as Petrified Garden, Banana Grove, and Paradise Lost.

The Bonneville Lock and Dam, located on the Columbia River between Oregon and Washington, has made it possible for boats to travel on a 465-mile waterway. Fish ladders allow migrating salmon to climb over the dam.

The viewing room beneath the dam is one of the most popular tourist attractions in the state. Visitors can watch through underwater windows as the fish move up a ladder. A nearby hatchery has made the area a popular fishing spot.

Hell's Canyon National Recreation Area offers rafting and some of the best fishing in the state. Trout, bass, catfish, sturgeon, and salmon can be pulled from the Snake River.

Over the centuries the Snake River has scraped a 7,913-foot gorge into He Devil Mountain. Hell's Canyon is the deepest gorge in North America. Today the steep canyon walls look down on swirling white-water rapids.

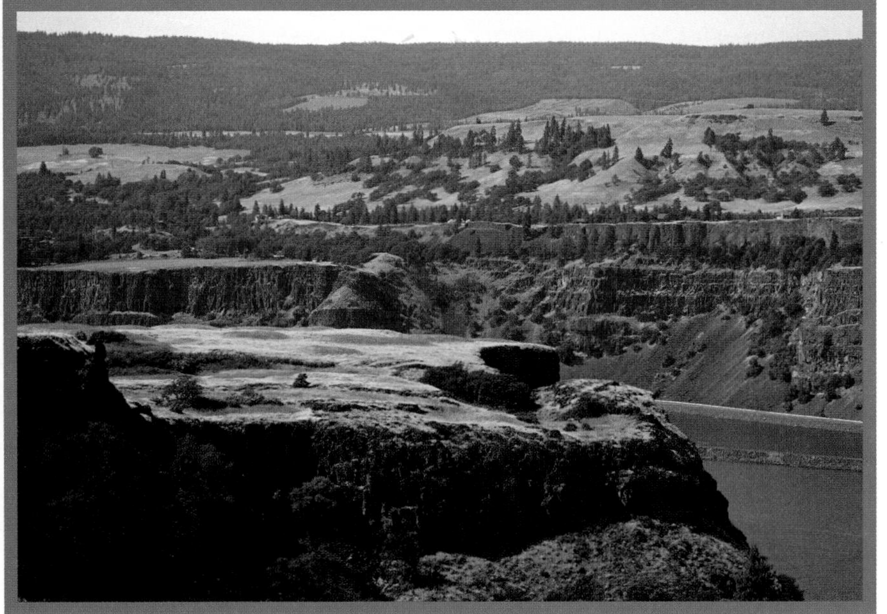

The Columbia River Gorge is the place where the Columbia River cuts through the Cascade Mountains.

Museums and Aquariums

The best place to see the state's famous fish is at the Oregon Coast Aquarium, in Newport. The gigantic aquarium covers six acres and holds more than ten thousand animals. Sturgeon and salmon highlight one of the largest displays.

One of the most beautiful sites in Oregon is Crater Lake National Park. The lake itself is famous for its bright blue water. It is surrounded by cliffs that reach 2,000 feet. Throughout much of the year, the cliffs and the nearby mountains are covered with snow.

For thousands of years, Mount Mazama, a 12,000-foot volcano, towered over what became southwestern Oregon. When all the lava had flowed out, the hollow mountain collapsed, leaving a giant crater. In the eight thousand years since the end of Mount Mazama, springs,

Crater Lake National Park is one of the most beautiful places to visit in Oregon. It is famous for its crystal clear water and snow-capped mountains.

rain, and melting snow have made a lake in the crater. Its 1,932-foot depth makes Crater Lake the deepest lake in the United States.

The most popular museum in the state is the Oregon Museum of Science and Industry, in Portland. It features hands-on exhibits. Visitors can touch a tornado and be shaken by a simulated earthquake. There is also a planetarium and a giant theater.

Chapter 3 ▶

Interesting Oregonians

Many important and interesting people have either been born in Oregon, or spent the bulk of their lives there. These are just a few.

John McLoughlin

American Indians trusted John McLoughlin. Because of his grey hair, they called him White Headed Eagle. He was a Canadian who worked for Britain's Hudson's Bay Company. When he was in charge of the company's fur-trading business, relations between the white trappers and the American Indians in Oregon were peaceful.

During the early 1800s, McLoughlin established twenty forts and trading posts. He also built saw mills and flour mills. Oregon lumber was exported to Alaska and Hawaii. The Hudson's Bay Company reaped huge profits.

Part of McLoughlin's job was to discourage settlement in Oregon. Too many white settlers would just upset the natives and take up too much land used for trapping. Worse than that, if too many Americans came to Oregon, the company feared the United States would take control of the area. Instead, McLoughlin encouraged and aided the early white settlers. He helped develop so much of the territory that today he is known as the Father of Oregon.

John Jacob Astor

John Jacob Astor left his home in Germany when he was just eighteen years old. When he arrived in New York City in 1784, he only had about fifty dollars.

John McLoughlin: "Father of Oregon" - Microsoft Internet Explorer

File Edit View Favorites Tools Help

Address http://arcweb.sos.state.or.us/50th/McLoughlin/mcloughlinintro.html

Oregon State Archives
50th Anniversary Exhibit

John McLoughlin: Father of Oregon

John McLoughlin meets Narcissa Whitman, the first white woman in Oregon, in 1836 (mural in the rotunda of the Oregon Capitol)

Done Internet

John McLoughlin was a Canadian-born trader who is often referred to as the Father of Oregon. He developed friendly relations with the American Indians because he respected their cultures and values.

Astor worked hard and two years later he was able to open a store where he sold musical instruments. He also bought and sold furs. Astor realized there was much more money to be made in furs than in instruments.

He established the American Fur Company, which would buy furs from the American frontier and sell them around the world.

The American Fur Company sent a ship to Oregon in 1811. Its crew built a fort and named it Astoria. The War of 1812 disrupted trade and forced Astor to sell Astoria.

Astoria was one of Astor's few ideas that did not make him richer. He bought furs throughout the American West, and then transported them to Asia and Europe on ships he owned. When he died in 1848, he was the richest man in the United States.

Jason Lee

Jason Lee met with little success as a missionary. In 1834, after he delivered his first sermon in Oregon, the mountain men and Indians celebrated with a horse race. Unfortunately, a rider fell off and was killed. The next day Lee conducted the first Protestant funeral in Oregon.

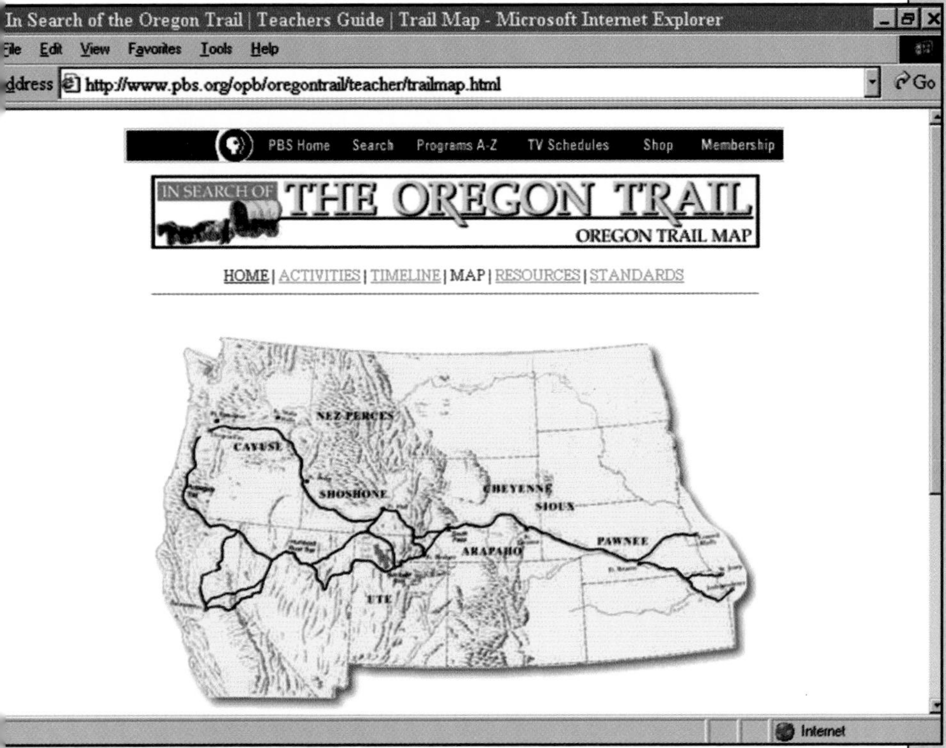

In Search of the Oregon Trail | Teachers Guide | Trail Map - Microsoft Internet Explorer
File Edit View Favorites Tools Help
Address http://www.pbs.org/opb/oregontrail/teacher/trailmap.html
PBS Home Search Programs A-Z TV Schedules Shop Membership
IN SEARCH OF THE OREGON TRAIL
OREGON TRAIL MAP
HOME | ACTIVITIES | TIMELINE | MAP | RESOURCES | STANDARDS
NEZ PERCES
CAYUSE
SHOSHONE
CHEYENNE
SIOUX
PAWNEE
ARAPAHO
UTE
Internet

This map shows the route that many Americans took to Oregon. It is known as the Oregon Trail.

Lee established a Christian school for American Indians at Mission Bottom. Out of fourteen students the first year, seven died and five ran away. The next year, sixteen of twenty-five died.

He had better luck encouraging settlers to come to Oregon. One of the men he brought was George Abernethy, who later became Oregon's first elected governor.

Lee established several Methodist churches for settlers. He also founded Salem, the state capital, and the Oregon Institute. It was the first university west of the Mississippi River. Today it is known as Willamette University.

Chief Joseph

His tribal name was Thunder Rolling Down the Mountain, but the great Nez Percé chief was better known as Joseph the Younger. His father was a baptized Christian known as Joseph the Elder. He signed a treaty with the American government guaranteeing the tribe a huge portion of Idaho and Oregon. However, when gold was discovered there, the government took back most of the land.

Joseph the Elder destroyed his Bible and his American flag. He said he would never leave the land. Joseph the Younger became chief when his father died in 1871. He, too, refused to leave the land that had been promised.

When United States troops threatened to attack, Chief Joseph led his tribe in a retreat to Canada. He hoped to join forces with Sioux Indians who lived there.

Of the seven hundred Nez Percé marching with Joseph, only about two hundred were warriors. Yet they managed to elude more than two thousand troops for three months. Even four battles along the way did not slow them down. Joseph and his people almost made it. They were

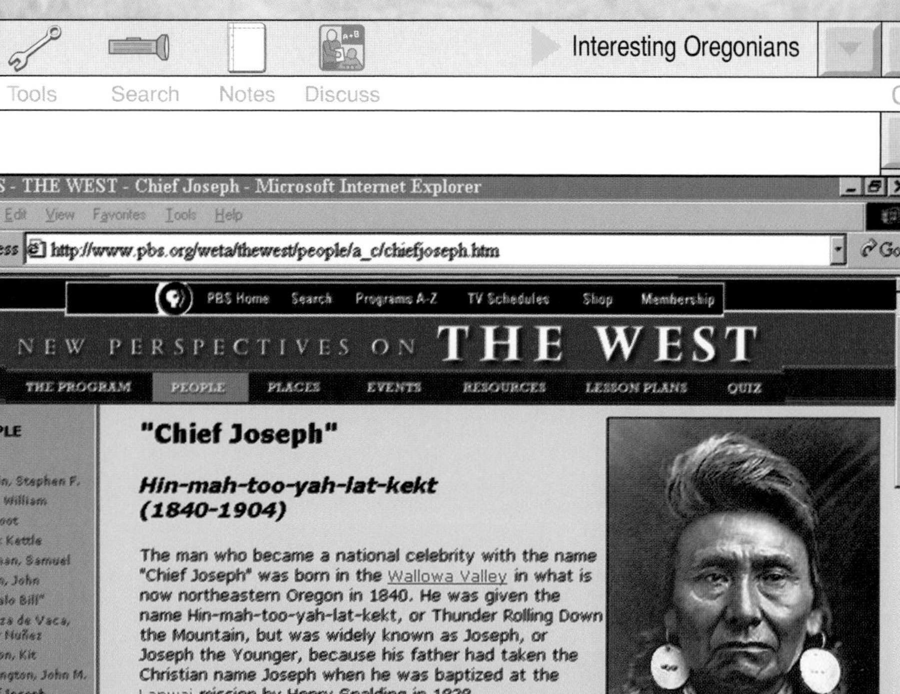

PBS - THE WEST - Chief Joseph - Microsoft Internet Explorer

http://www.pbs.org/weta/thewest/people/a_c/chiefjoseph.htm

PBS Home Search Programs A-Z TV Schedules Shop Membership

NEW PERSPECTIVES ON THE WEST

THE PROGRAM PEOPLE PLACES EVENTS RESOURCES LESSON PLANS QUIZ

"Chief Joseph"

Hin-mah-too-yah-lat-kekt (1840-1904)

The man who became a national celebrity with the name "Chief Joseph" was born in the Wallowa Valley in what is now northeastern Oregon in 1840. He was given the name Hin-mah-too-yah-lat-kekt, or Thunder Rolling Down the Mountain, but was widely known as Joseph, or Joseph the Younger, because his father had taken the Christian name Joseph when he was baptized at the Lapwai mission by Henry Spalding in 1838.

Joseph the Elder was one of the first Nez Percé converts to Christianity and an active supporter of the tribe's longstanding peace with whites. In 1855 he even helped Washington's territorial governor set up a Nez Percé reservation that stretched from Oregon into Idaho. But in 1863, following a gold rush into Nez Percé territory, the federal government took back almost six million acres of this land, restricting the Nez Percé to a reservation in Idaho that was only one tenth its prior size. Feeling himself betrayed, Joseph the Elder denounced the United States, destroyed his American

After Chief Joseph's band and United States troops engaged in war, Joseph's troops were forced to surrender. As a result, the U.S. government forced them to relocate to present-day Oklahoma.

only forty miles from the Canadian border when they were surrounded and forced to surrender.

When at last he gave up the fight, Chief Joseph delivered one of the most famous speeches in American history. "I am tired of fighting. Our chiefs are killed . . . It is cold and we have no blankets. The little children are freezing to death . . . My heart is sick and sad. From where the sun now stands I will fight no more forever."[1]

Joseph and his people were forced to move to the Indian Territory in what is now Oklahoma. He never returned to Oregon.

Abigail Scott Duniway

Abigail married Benjamin C. Duniway in 1853. She probably would have lived a quiet life as a farmer's wife and the mother of six children, but nine years later, Benjamin was injured in an accident and could no longer work. It was then up to Abigail to support the family.

She ran a hat shop in Albany for several years. In 1871, the Duniways moved to Portland, where she published *The New Northwest.* As a woman running a business, Abigail encountered many problems. She decided that most of the unfair treatment would end if women could vote.

Abigail demanded suffrage and equal rights for women in her newspaper. Her crusade helped women win the vote

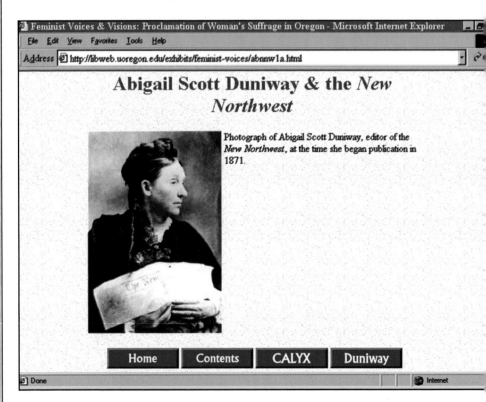

Abigail Scott Duniway advocated for equal rights and suffrage for women.

in Idaho, Washington, and Oregon. Duniway herself cast her first vote in 1916, when she was sixty-three years of age.

Linus Pauling

When Linus Pauling was in high school in Portland, he decided, "The important thing is to have many ideas."[2] Throughout his long career as a chemist and a humanitarian, he followed his own advice.

Pauling shot X-rays through crystals to determine how atoms are linked, or bonded. He discovered the structure of amino acids, which are the building blocks of protein. His work helped doctors begin to understand sickle-cell anemia, a serious blood disease.

Pauling crusaded against the testing of nuclear weapons. More than eleven thousand scientists from forty-nine nations signed his petition against such testing. His efforts helped lead to the Nuclear Test Ban Treaty in 1963.

Pauling was awarded two Nobel Prizes, one for chemistry in 1954 and the other for peace in 1962.

Maurine Neuberger

Maurine and Richard Neuberger were both interested in politics. She taught physical education and English at Lincoln High School in Portland. He was a journalist. In 1948, he was elected to the Oregon state senate. Two years later, they became a legislative couple when she was elected to the Oregon house of representatives. "My husband and I have found it a great asset to work as a team," she said.[3]

Maurine was criticized by some people who claimed that a woman's place was in the home. "It's a woman's world as well as a man's world," she said.[4] When the couple ran for reelection in 1952, she got more votes.

They campaigned together two years later when

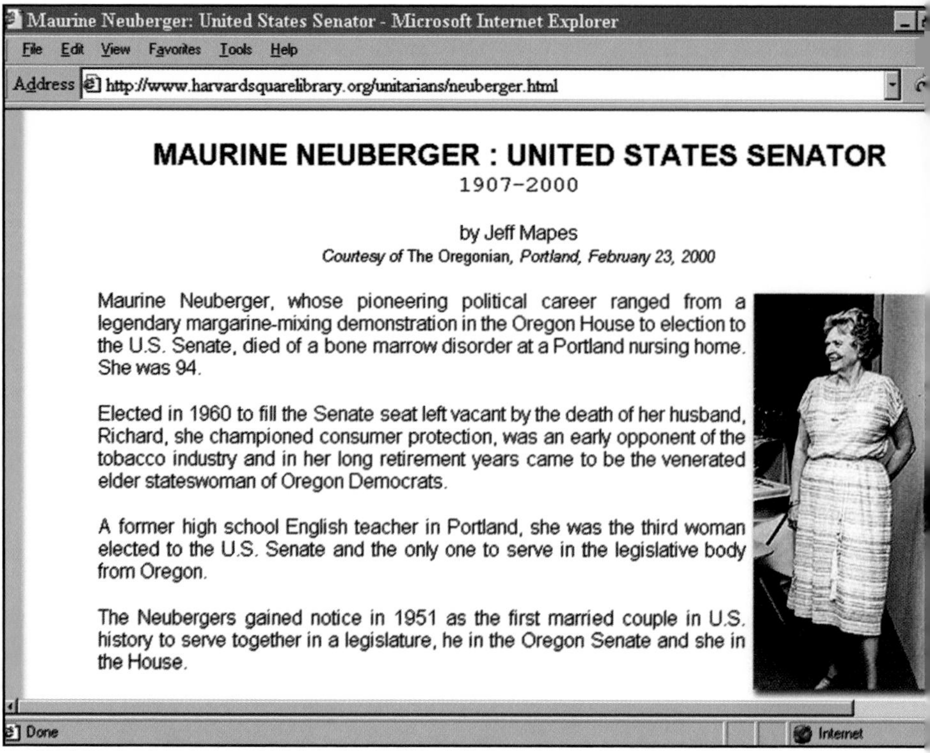

Maurine Neuberger: United States Senator - Microsoft Internet Explorer

Address http://www.harvardsquarelibrary.org/unitarians/neuberger.html

MAURINE NEUBERGER : UNITED STATES SENATOR
1907–2000

by Jeff Mapes
Courtesy of The Oregonian, *Portland, February 23, 2000*

Maurine Neuberger, whose pioneering political career ranged from a legendary margarine-mixing demonstration in the Oregon House to election to the U.S. Senate, died of a bone marrow disorder at a Portland nursing home. She was 94.

Elected in 1960 to fill the Senate seat left vacant by the death of her husband, Richard, she championed consumer protection, was an early opponent of the tobacco industry and in her long retirement years came to be the venerated elder stateswoman of Oregon Democrats.

A former high school English teacher in Portland, she was the third woman elected to the U.S. Senate and the only one to serve in the legislative body from Oregon.

The Neubergers gained notice in 1951 as the first married couple in U.S. history to serve together in a legislature, he in the Oregon Senate and she in the House.

Done Internet

Maurine Neuberger was one of the nation's first woman senators. She challenged the views of many people who felt that "a woman's place was in the home."

Richard ran for the United States Senate. He was elected and they moved to Washington, D.C. When Richard died in 1960, Maurine ran for the seat—and won.

When she took office, Neuberger was one of only two women in the Senate. As a senator, she was one of the first to call for antipollution devices on automobiles. She wrote a book attacking tobacco companies and campaigned for the first warning labels on cigarettes.

Ken Kesey

Ken Kesey was an Oregonian with unusual, unpopular ideas. In 1962, Kesey wrote *One Flew Over the*

Cuckoo's Nest, a strange novel about patients in a psychiatric hospital, and one man's struggle to stand up against society. It became a popular play and then, in 1975, one of the most-honored motion pictures of all time.

It was Kesey's other ideas, not his book, that got him into trouble. He argued that drugs such as LSD could help people think more clearly and enjoy life more fully. The authorities and most of the population did not agree. Kesey served time in jail for violating drug laws. He only wrote two more books before his death in 2001.

Improving the Sneaker

Back in the 1960s, Bill Bowerman, a track coach at the University of Oregon, had a problem with sneakers. He thought they were too heavy. Every ounce he could cut off the weight of a shoe, he figured, would mean 200 less pounds lifted by a runner in a mile-long race. Still, he was not sure how to cut the weight. One morning while eating waffles for breakfast, Bowerman figured it out. Soon he was pouring hot rubber into his wife's waffle maker and making his own shoes.

Bowerman used his homemade shoes for his runners at the University of Oregon. He teamed up with Phil Knight, one of his former runners, to sell the shoes throughout the country. Together they formed Blue Ribbon Sports.

The company did phenomenally well. In 1972, Knight changed its name to Nike. In the 1980s, he hired Jordan to advertise his shoes. Suddenly the shoes were "cool."

Over the years, Nike has been criticized for its high prices and for paying foreign workers low wages to make its products, but it remains one of Oregon's most popular and successful companies.

Back Forward Stop Review Home Explore Favorites History

Chapter 4

Government and Economy

Oregon's cities and towns have home rule. This means that their voters can choose the form of government they prefer. Most of the towns have a mayor and a council. The cities have almost all chosen to have an appointed city manager and an elected council. The state has thirty-six counties. Most are governed by boards of commissioners.

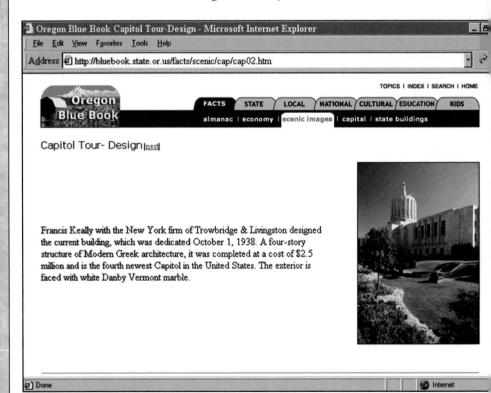

Oregon Blue Book Capitol Tour-Design - Microsoft Internet Explorer

File Edit View Favorites Tools Help

Address http://bluebook.state.or.us/facts/scenic/cap/cap02.htm

TOPICS | INDEX | SEARCH | HOME

Oregon Blue Book

FACTS STATE LOCAL NATIONAL CULTURAL EDUCATION KIDS

almanac | economy | scenic images | capital | state buildings

Capitol Tour- Design |next|

Francis Keally with the New York firm of Trowbridge & Livingston designed the current building, which was dedicated October 1, 1938. A four-story structure of Modern Greek architecture, it was completed at a cost of $2.5 million and is the fourth newest Capitol in the United States. The exterior is faced with white Danby Vermont marble.

Done Internet

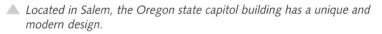

▲ *Located in Salem, the Oregon state capitol building has a unique and modern design.*

Running the State

Like the United States Constitution, Oregon's constitution divides power between executive, legislative, and judicial branches. The state constitution has been in effect since 1857, two years before Oregon joined the Union.

The governor heads the executive branch and serves a four-year term. He or she appoints many state officials. Oregon's first thirty-three governors were men. Then Barbara Roberts was elected in 1990.

The Legislative Assembly is composed of the senate, with thirty members, and the house of representatives, with sixty members. Together the two bodies vote on laws for the state.

Oregon's judicial branch is headed by the state Supreme Court. Its seven justices are the final appeals court for state matters. The state also has ten judges on the court of appeals and nineteen other judicial districts. All justices and judges are elected.

Half of the state's budget is funded by a personal income tax. There are also state taxes on gasoline and tobacco. A state lottery supplies additional funds.

The State Capital

Salem got its start because missionary Jason Lee needed cash to finance his school. He picked a spot for a town in western Oregon, then divided the land into lots. When he sold the lots, the money helped keep his Oregon Institute running.

The Calapooya Indian name for the site was Chemeketa, or place of rest. However, the missionaries picked a new name from the Bible. Salem means peace. Salem became the state capital in 1855.

The capitol building in Salem is an interesting structure with a modern design. Instead of a dome, the tower in the middle is topped by a golden statue representing the pioneers who settled Oregon.

Employment

Like people in other states, most workers in Oregon are employed in service industries. They work for the government (local, state, or national), or are employed by businesses such as stores, restaurants, hospitals, insurance companies, or real estate agencies.

Luckily for Oregon, almost half of the state is covered

Oregon Blue Book-Work: Log Wagon - Microsoft Internet Explorer
File Edit View Favorites Tools Help
Address http://bluebook.state.or.us/facts/scenic/work/logwagon.htm
TOPICS | INDEX | SEARCH | HOME
Oregon Blue Book
FACTS STATE LOCAL NATIONAL CULTURAL EDUCATION KIDS
almanac | economy | scenic images | capital | state buildings
Oregon at Work | next |

Log hauling in Hood River County. (Hood River County Museum)

| Oregon at Work home | next |

Internet

Since the state of Oregon is covered with forests, wood production remains the most important industry.

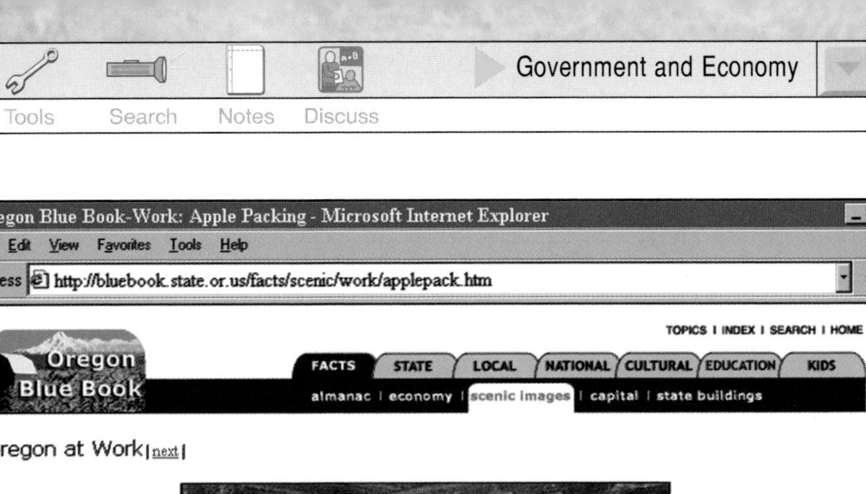

Workers boxing apples in Hood River County (Hood River County Museum)

Apple packing has long been an important industry in Oregon. In this photo, workers are packing apples in boxes in Hood River County in the 1900s.

with forests. Its most important timber trees are the Douglas fir and the ponderosa pine. Oregon has produced more lumber than any other state every year since 1938. It is not surprising that the forest-products industry is Oregon's biggest employer.

Workers must care for the trees, cut them down, and then replant new ones. Saw mills cut the lumber into boards. Processing plants produce plywood and particleboard. Other workers are involved in shipping wood products all over the world.

The food processing industry is second only to forest products. Have you ever eaten french fries made from precut, frozen potatoes? Chances are that many of them came from Oregon. Frozen fruits and other vegetables are also processed in big factories.

On the state's thirty-six thousand farms, important crops are wheat and hay. In the eastern part of the state near Idaho, millions of potatoes are grown each year. Farms in the western part of the state produce flowers such as tulips, daffodils, and lilies so they can sell the bulbs. Oregon's orchards produce pears, apples, and sweet cherries.

Chapter 5 ▶

History

On the wall of a cave near Fort Rock, there is a faded picture of a man with a spear. This is some of the earliest evidence of human life in the area that became Oregon. Scientists believe there were people there at least ten thousand years ago. Archaeologists cannot tell us much more than that. These mysterious people left no monuments or ruins. Only the painting and a few small artifacts have been left behind.

American Indians

Much more is known about the American Indians who lived in Oregon before white explorers and settlers arrived. The Chinook lived in fishing villages near the mouth of the Columbia River. They traveled in beautiful canoes carved from cedar wood. They survived by fishing and gathering foods such as berries, nuts, and roots. They also traded with other tribes. One of their traditions was a giant feast called a potlatch.

In southwestern Oregon, the Klamath and Modoc used marsh plants to make baskets and much of their clothing. In the winter, they lived in lodges built in pits with wood, and covered with dirt. Their wickiups, or thin shelters covered with reed mats, were home in the summer. For food, they fished, hunted, and gathered wild vegetables.

The Nez Percé lived in northeastern Oregon. Their name is French for pierced nose. A trapper gave them

the name when he saw a few of them wearing shell decorations on their noses. They did much trading with other tribes. They were the first people in Oregon to have horses. By carefully breeding the animals, they developed horses that were especially fast.

The Paiute and Cayuse lived in eastern Oregon in pointed houses with walls made of brush. Not much grew on their dry land, so they were sometimes forced to eat mice, insects, and jackrabbits.

European Explorers

The first Europeans who came to Oregon were looking for a shortcut. In the 1540s, Bartolomé Ferrelo and his Spanish sailors were probably the first whites to see the Oregon coast. They were looking for a river that would lead across North America and back to Europe.

Sir Francis Drake was looking for the same thing in 1579. He called it the Northwest Passage. Unfortunately for the sailors, there was no such thing. To get from one ocean to the other, they would have to sail around the southern tip of South America.

Two hundred years later, when George Washington was president of the United States, Robert Gray's crew became the first Americans to see Oregon. In 1792, he sailed into a large river and named it Columbia after his ship.

The first thorough exploration of the area came in 1805. Meriwether Lewis and William Clark had been sent by President Thomas Jefferson to explore the land gained from the Louisiana Purchase. Lewis and Clark explored beyond the Louisiana Territory, looking for the Pacific Ocean. With the help of the Nez Percé, they made it, paddling their canoes to the mouth of the Columbia River.

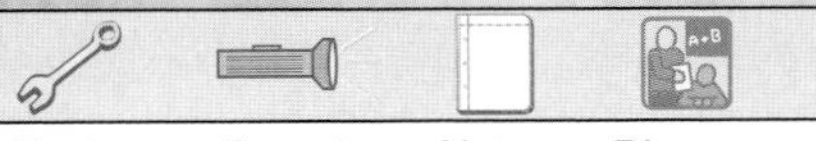

Who Owned Oregon?

By the time of the Lewis and Clark Expedition, four countries claimed at least part of the Oregon country—Great Britain, Russia, Spain, and the United States.

British ships sailed the Columbia River soon after the visit by American Robert Gray. Their fur traders conducted business with the American Indians throughout the area. Russia had explored farther north in Alaska. The Spanish claim was based on Bartolomé Ferrelo's voyage and their settlements farther south in California.

In a series of treaties, Russia and Spain eventually gave up their claims. Britain and the United States could not

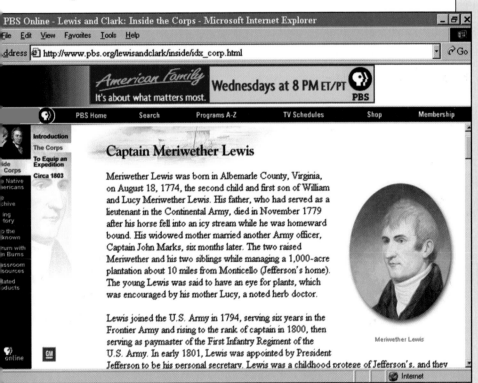

PBS Online - Lewis and Clark: Inside the Corps - Microsoft Internet Explorer

File Edit View Favorites Tools Help

Address http://www.pbs.org/lewisandclark/inside/idx_corp.html Go

PBS Home Search Programs A-Z TV Schedules Shop Membership

Introduction
The Corps
To Equip an Expedition
Circa 1803

Captain Meriwether Lewis

Meriwether Lewis was born in Albemarle County, Virginia, on August 18, 1774, the second child and first son of William and Lucy Meriwether Lewis. His father, who had served as a lieutenant in the Continental Army, died in November 1779 after his horse fell into an icy stream while he was homeward bound. His widowed mother married another Army officer, Captain John Marks, six months later. The two raised Meriwether and his two siblings while managing a 1,000-acre plantation about 10 miles from Monticello (Jefferson's home). The young Lewis was said to have an eye for plants, which was encouraged by his mother Lucy, a noted herb doctor.

Meriwether Lewis

Lewis joined the U.S. Army in 1794, serving six years in the Frontier Army and rising to the rank of captain in 1800, then serving as paymaster of the First Infantry Regiment of the U.S. Army. In early 1801, Lewis was appointed by President Jefferson to be his personal secretary. Lewis was a childhood protege of Jefferson's, and they

Internet

Captain Meriwether Lewis was an American explorer. President Thomas Jefferson asked Lewis to explore a route west to the Pacific Coast. Lewis asked Captain William Clark to join him.

agree on a boundary between Canada and the western American territory. They finally agreed to allow citizens of both countries to live and work in Oregon.

Oregon Fever

The Lewis and Clark Expedition fascinated Americans. Their journals encouraged a few others to travel to Oregon. They bought back wonderful stories about beautiful mountains and rivers, wonderful soil for crops, and plentiful fish and game. It was a wide-open, almost empty territory. The American Indians there seemed to get along with the whites.

PBS Online - Lewis and Clark: Inside the Corps - Microsoft Internet Explorer

File Edit View Favorites Tools Help

Address http://www.pbs.org/lewisandclark/inside/idx_corp.html

American Family It's about what matters most. Wednesdays at 8 PM ET/PT PBS

PBS Home Search Programs A-Z TV Schedules Shop Membership

Introduction
The Corps
To Equip an Expedition
Circa 1803

Inside the Corps
The Native Americans
The Archive
Living History
Into the Unknown
Forum with Ken Burns
Classroom Resources
Related Products

Captain William Clark

Captain William Clark, the red-haired co-captain of the Corps of Discovery, was born on August 1, 1770, the sixth son and ninth child from a family of 10 children. Originally from the same area of Virginia that was home to both Jefferson and Lewis, Clark's parents relocated their family near the Rappahannock River, where William was born. All of Clark's brothers were Revolutionary War veterans, including the famed George Rogers Clark, who commanded Virginia's troops in the Kentucky region during Jefferson's term as Virginia governor. After the War was over, the Clark family migrated across the Allegheny Mountains and down the Ohio River to Mulberry Hill, near Louisville. Clark learned about wilderness skills and natural history from his older brother, George.

William Clark

Clark began his military career at age 19 when he joined the Kentucky Militia. He later joined the regular army and was promoted to lieutenant. During this

online GM Internet

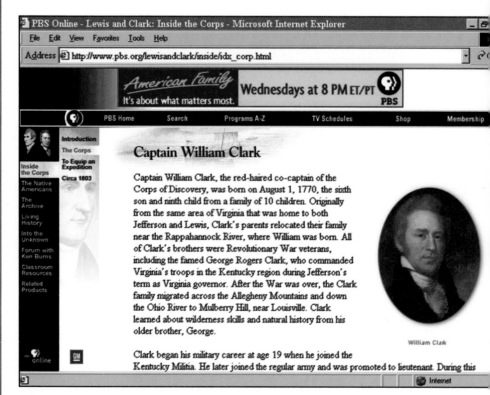

Captain William Clark, along with Meriwether Lewis, led the famous Lewis and Clark expedition.

Other Americans in the east were concerned about the souls of American Indians. They were not really bothered that white settlers would soon be taking huge chunks of Indian lands. They were only interested in converting American Indians to Christianity. The missionaries packed up their Bibles and headed for Oregon.

Oregon Trail

The problem was getting to the territory. Most Americans lived on the other side of the continent. It was almost as close to Hawaii as it was to New York City. The easiest way to get there from America's Atlantic Coast was by ship, but the trip took months and was far too expensive for most settlers.

For almost everybody going to Oregon, the only way to get there was by walking alongside a covered wagon. After reaching Independence, Missouri, there were no roads, only a rough trail that stretched 2,000 miles westward. It followed rivers across the present states of Kansas, Nebraska, Wyoming, and Idaho.

Flooded rivers. Rocky cliffs. Diseases with no medicines or doctors to help. Steep mountains. Deserts. Sometimes no fresh water or firewood for weeks. Almost six months were required to cover the trail. During the fifty years after 1830, almost 500,000 men, women, and children tried to make the journey. About thirty-four thousand died on the way.

Americans Take Over

Scattered groups began to arrive in John McLoughlin's Oregon territory. By 1840, there were at least seven missions seeking to convert Indians. The first large group of

settlers, about nine hundred of them, made it over the Oregon Trail in 1843. Hundreds more arrived every year.

As a Canadian working for the British Hudson's Bay Company, McLoughlin was supposed to discourage American settlement. Instead, he welcomed them, giving them advice and sometimes even money.

Because he failed to keep the Americans out, McLoughlin eventually lost his job. By then, the British could do little to keep control of the territory. They were vastly outnumbered by the Americans and hundreds more were always on the way. In 1846, Great Britain and the United States agreed on the border. Oregon now belonged to the Americans.

American Indians Strike Back

The various tribes got along well with the fur traders and early settlers. A few even converted to Christianity; the white man's religion. However, as more and more settlers arrived, the American Indians saw more and more of their land being taken away. Unfamiliar diseases such as measles killed thousands.

In 1847, Cayuse Indians took their revenge on Marcus and Narcissa Whitman, a missionary couple. Chief Tiloukaikt led a raiding party that killed the Whitmans and twelve other whites, then burned their mission. Americans called it the Whitman Massacre.

United States troops battered the Cayuse for the next two years until Tiloukaikt surrendered. He hoped that by giving himself up he could convince the United States to let his people continue to live in Oregon. Just before he and five other Cayuse were hanged, he said, "Did not your missionaries teach us that Christ died to save his people? So we die to save our people."[1]

The Whitmans were missionaries who came to Oregon to convert American Indians to Christianity. The Cayuse Indians killed the Whitmans in 1847 after blaming them for a measles epidemic that took the lives of the Cayuse children.

When gold was discovered a few years later, settlers pushed even more natives off their land. Fighting continued until all American Indians in that area were moved to a reservation in 1856.

When the Madoc Indians were forced onto a reservation in 1872, they escaped and hid along Oregon's southern border with California. After a long siege, the Madoc surrendered and were taken back to the reservation.

Five years later it was the turn of the Nez Percé to give up their land. Instead of moving his people to the assigned reservation, Chief Joseph led them toward Canada. He and

200 warriors, accompanied by 500 women, old people, and children, outwitted troops for several months. They made it out of Oregon, through Idaho, and into Montana before they were captured and sent to their reservation in Oklahoma.

Chief Joseph gave the American settlers advice they did not follow:

> If the white man wants to live in peace with the Indian . . . we can live in peace . . . Treat all men alike . . . give them all the same law . . . Let me be a free man . . . free to travel . . . free to work . . . free to choose my own teachers . . . free to follow the religion of my fathers . . . free to think and talk and act for myself.[2]

The Thirty-Third State

The Oregon Donation Land Law, passed by Congress in 1850, encouraged even more Americans to come to Oregon. According to the law, settlers could receive 320 acres of land if they promised to grow crops on it for four years.

By 1859, there were about fifty thousand whites living in the territory. That was the year Oregon became the thirty-third state in the Union. Even more people came after the Civil War ended in 1865. By then, they could use railroads for at least part of the journey. In 1883, Oregon was connected to the transcontinental railroad system. In 1890, the state's population was more than 300,000.

The Oregon System

In the early years of the twentieth century, Oregon gained a reputation as a place where citizens were not afraid to try new ideas. In 1902, the state adopted the initiative and referendum. The new rules allowed voters, not just the legislature, to enact or do away with laws themselves. If enough people signed a petition, the voters of the state could decide whether or not to approve a law.

Six years later, Oregon voters got the power to recall public officials. If they did not approve of a public official's job performance, he or she could be voted out of office even before the term was over.

Initiative, referendum, and recall became known as the Oregon System. Together they gave direct power to the voters instead of reserving it for office holders. Soon other states adopted all or part of the Oregon System.

Protecting the Environment

Tom McCall was elected governor in 1966 after promising to fight against air and water pollution. New laws benefited the Willamette River. When pollution was curtailed, salmon returned to the river for the first time in dozens of years.

Oregon was also one of the first states to require a deposit on all drinks sold in cans or bottles. This encouraged people to recycle cans and bottles, and not to litter.

Oregonians have continued in the spirit of the early pioneers. Its people have been leaders in conserving natural resources and protecting the environment. For example, Senator Charles L. McNary was one of the first to push for expanding national forests and replanting trees cut for lumber. Those are the kinds of actions that have proven that Oregon has "a beloved place in the lives of its residents who enjoy sharing their history, products, and beauty with others."[3]

Oregon Facts

1. *USA State Symbols*, Flags & Facts, CD-ROM, Canada: Robesus, Inc., 2001.

Chapter 3. Interesting Oregonians

1. PBS, *New Perspectives on the West*, 2001, <http://www.pbs.org/weta/thewest/people/a_c/chiefjoseph.htm> (Jan. 15, 2002).

2. Gail Thompson and R. Andrew Viruleg, "Linus Pauling: A Biography," n.d., <http://www.woodrow.org/teachers/chemistry/institutes/1992/Pauling.html> (Jan. 15, 2002).

3. Jeff Mapes, "Maurine Neuberger: United States Senator," *Notable American Unitarians*, n.d., <http://www.harvardsquarelibrary.org/unitarians/neuberger.html> (Jan. 15, 2002).

4. Ibid.

Chapter 5. History

1. PBS, "Marcus Whitman (1802–1847) and Narcissa Whitman (1808–1847)," 2001, *New Perspectives on the West*, <http://www.pbs.org/weta/thewest/people/s_z/whitman.htm> (Jan. 15, 2002).

2. StoneE Producktions, "Chief Joseph Nez Percé (Nimiputimt)," 2000, *Stonee's Native Quotes*, <http://www.ilhawaii.net/~stony/joseph.html> (Jan. 15, 2002).

3. *USA State Symbols, Flags & Facts*, CD-ROM, Canada: Robesus, Inc., 2001.

Further Reading

Aylesworth, Thomas G. and Virginia L. Aylesworth. *The Northwest: Alaska, Idaho, Oregon, Washington.* Broomall, Pa.: Chelsea House Publishers, 1995.

Blackwood, Gary L. *Life on the Oregon Trail.* Farmington Hills, Mich.: Gale Group, 1999.

Cushing, Caleb. *Beyond the Rocky Mountains: Report on the Territory of Oregon.* Sharon, Mass.: Ye Galleon Press, 2000.

Ingram, Scott. *Oregon.* Second ed. Danbury, Conn.: Children's Press, 2000.

Rau, Dana Meachen. *Life on the Oregon Trail.* Farmington Hills, Mich.: Gale Group, 2001.

Ruby, Robert H. and John A. Brown. *The Cayuse Indians: Imperial Tribesmen of Old Oregon.* Seattle, Wash.: Northwest Interpretive Association, 1989.

Sanders, Richard S. *Government in Oregon.* Portland, Oreg.: M E S D Press, 1991.

Stickney, Joy. *Native Americans along the Oregon Trail.* Husum, Wash.: Canyon Creations, 1993.

Thompson, Kathleen. *Oregon.* Austin, Tex.: Raintree Steck-Vaughn Publishers, 1996.

Twiss, Travers. *Oregon Territory: Its History & Discovery.* Sharon, Mass.: Ye Galleon Press, 1998.

Walker, Dale L. *Pacific Destiny: The Three Hundred Year Journey to the Oregon Country.* New York: Tom Doherty Associates, LLC, 2000.

Wills, Charles A. *A Historical Album of Oregon.* Brookfield, Conn.: Millbrook Press, Inc., 1995.

Index